From Within

From Within

By Angela Ruth

Cover design by Emma R. and Angela Ruth
Illustrations by Roxanne Theresa

To my daughter Jasmine; my loved ones who call me Nana: Unique, Raymani, Robyn, Kaylani, Kristina, Alaynah, Ezra, Aria, Phillip; and my little sister forever, Nina.

TABLE OF CONTENTS   Page

ACKNOWLEDGEMENTS

It would be remiss of me if I did not acknowledge that the primary motivation was my mother's consistent encouragement over the years to continue writing and publish a book. Though no longer with us, it warms my heart reflecting on how happy, excited, and proud she would have been to see it finally become a reality.

My heartfelt appreciation to my Zoom poetry sisters and QH, our poet virtuoso for their poetic critical ear, inspiration, and warm rapport. Emma R and Roxanne Theresa for their artistic collaboration and patience, my daughter Jasmine and firstborn granddaughter Unique for their support, assistance with editing, and excited approval. My dear friend, Melissa Zaroia, may not be aware of how much she helped me through moments of hidden tears, and transition my feelings of apprehension to positive anticipation and accomplishment.

INTRODUCTION

A thought, a feeling. an observation, an experience

Write it!

PLEASANT THOUGHTS AND MEMORIES

My Peaceful Place

Comfortable, relaxed, stretched out on a warm bed of sand,
the wind embraces and massages like an invisible hand.
The great luminary above is a blinding and protective tower,
its' strength against my skin slowly siphons my power.
Confiscating the moisture beyond my lips,
I reach for my sparkling water at my fingertips.
Finally, a time to renew and refresh,
as the beauty of creation and my senses mesh.

Memories

A gentle touch from the wind,
a familiar feeling.
The sound of music
flows through the air,
my face smiles,
I start to reminisce.
A drifting scent of food,
I tasted it before.
A floating hint of cologne
Stirs up thoughts and feelings,
from somewhere,
about someone.

The Fashion Show

They stand with pride, strong and tall
survived another cold season after fall.
Their clothes were removed, bodies left bare
confident models unconcerned about what to wear.

Winter glides in crisp and cool,
powdering trees with sparkling jewels.
It melts in the ground then floats as mist in the air;
All that faded away begins to reappear.

An incomparable designer, in fact, supreme
will present to the world, the season's next theme.
The perfect shade of green coats the endless runways
the stage brightly lit by the magnificent sunrays.

The decorative arrangement of flowers perfectly pigmented;
A work no human could accomplish; this was masterfully invented.
The music begins with the melodious harmony of birds,
the highest quality of sound effects, to describe are no words.

With the wind the models move in rhythmical fashion,
the array of beautiful colors, create an awestruck reaction.
The fashion show does not discriminate it is free and for all to see
The models are the tiniest flowers to the most luxuriant tree.

The next time when walking, running, or driving outside,
take notice of the Creator's fashion show displayed earth-wide.

The Sting

It was some time ago when we first met,
No mutual interest, at least not yet.
I heard stories about you from one person or another,
And stood at a distance when you spent time with my brother.
It didn't seem you really wanted to be his friend,
But genuine hospitality he would regularly extend.
However, after much time had passed,
we ran into each other at last.
Older now, and somewhat reserved,
by your presence I was a bit unnerved.
It was an encounter short and sweet,
Nothing eventful, no plans again to meet.

But it seemed everywhere I attended an event,
You would show up, I wondered your true intent.
I noticed at the oddest places you would appear,
and made it obvious to me that you were there.
While your advances I managed to avoid,
your persistence caused me to become
increasingly paranoid.

The situation needed to be defined,
No more walks on a beautiful day
without looking behind.
Could it be, for what you're searching is not me,
Though, I'm convinced there is mischief to a
great degree?

My hope was eventually you would withdraw,

I accepted my feelings were not facts and
you broke no law.

Then came what I had for so long dreaded,
I saw you, then to me you immediately headed.
I tried not to panic and attempted to slip away.
But you seized the perfect opportunity
and stung me that day.
For those who I have not told or do not know me,
This story is about my warm weather stalker,
the bee.

Our Special Event

The night of the announcement, the location all would know,
There is never a question if we will or should go.
I have to think about what to wear,
Should I braid, curl or straighten my hair.
Yes, preparing for this event is really exciting,
Soon we'll be thinking about those we will be inviting.
Oh my, it's May already and how time soared?
And I need to go quickly to the sewing supply store.
I want to wear something my own unique style,
with all day comfort, contributing to a serene smile.
I'll make a few dresses with the same color theme,
It's now a week away have to create those seams
Now I'm thinking.... there's not much time,
But, it will be okay, the challenge is all mine.
A week later we arrived at the event site,
Our family of six dressed in colors so bright.
The combined colors of yellow, white and gray
I couldn't believe I made it happen by this day.

Remember The Days?

Waking from sleep, still in a daze,
I started to drift off and remember the days.
When the only phone in every home was a landline,
and we never formed a line to use it in our family of nine.
My parents made sure we always had a dime,
to use the public pay phones if we wouldn't be home in time.
And we had to eat all the food on our plate and not waste,
But that rule made it hard for this girl to stay slim around the waist.
I remember shopping without much money but there was always a way,
I could purchase that special something with a few dollars on layaway.
And remember when commercials advertised soap lathered in a shower,
and after the body is smell good clean use a little powder?
Today, it seems the trend is to skip that process,
with products that keep the body all day fresh.
Now in my household we learned many a lesson,
with good training so problems in the future would lessen.
I would have been in big trouble if I called my parents "bruh" or "bro"
Especially to the one whose womb housed me when a developing embryo.
She would have absolutely viewed this as an attempt to defy her,
And when did something cool and amazing

become the same as heat and flames, “fire?”
Pardon me I think I drifted from remember
the days and went off on a tangent,
forgetting everything in this world is transient.

My Most Embarassing Moment

I remember one time I was as excited as could be,
I purchased concert tickets for my niece and me.
We went to the beautiful music hall,
My chance to walk elegant and tall.

Oh the dilemma of what to wear,
a classy look my attire had to declare.
And there she was my fuschia chiffon dress,
Searching for this garment, left my closet a mess.
My jewelry elevated the look without being too much,
Then I sealed it with patent leather pumps and matching
clutch.

The show was incredible and we gave the performance a
standing ovation,
Then it concluded with everyone exiting on the red carpet,
the second sensation.
I held my bag in model fashion, underneath my arm
Confident I carried myself with grace and charm.

After a few steps, I realized my heel was caught in a carpet
snag,
My left arm swung forward while my right still held my bag.
My body fought violently to catch itself and regain control,
But I tripped endlessly down the carpet instead of a model's
stroll.
I finally regained my composure and in a panic ran out,
Embarassed and humiliated without a doubt.
A good lesson in a public display of conceit,
I'll always remember but never want to repeat.

Blue Serenity

I look up and see your beauty,
No paint or crayon can accurately portray,
You've been labeled as powder, sky, and baby.
You are in a class of your own.
If I played you on my piano.
Soothing the melody would be
The song title, Blue Serenity.

Unexpected

Four, twenty-eight, twenty-three,
An end of a life we did not foresee.
One, zero, three, nine,
The doctor's pronouncement embedded in the mind.
Seven, six, five, four,
Sisters remaining, the brothers are no more.
Mother standing by his side,
Never imagined a third son would die.
Family hurting, more than a few,
From the oldest sibling to the youngest nephew.
All shocked and deeply sad,
Who knew it was stage 4 cancer he had?
He would often worry about his health in excess,
Playing doctor, would try to interpret his own tests.
But this time, his condition was serious and real,
How can we help him through this ordeal.
Many thanks to his spiritual mentor and friend,
who assisted and supported him until the end.

Though Silent She Speaks

She demonstrated how a woman should be,
All that she was, I want in me.
The way she spoke, listened and the time spent.
Invaluable and still training me at present.
When troubled I reflect on her reminders and advice
Always thought provoking, wise, and concise.

Because though silent she speaks.

She displayed such beautiful qualities,
Led a balanced life, clear of her priorities.
I miss my dear friend, confidant, and mother,
I'm still being trained by all I learned from her.

Yes, though silent, she speaks.

My Shannon

From an infant to a teenager, she was quiet and shy,
The most she would say was a soft "hi" or "bye."
As she grew up and the years passed by
She became the girl with the signature peace sign and
melodious hiii!
She brightened the room with her laughter and sparkling
smile,
Always fashionable with her own unique style.
Her favorite songs were about needing reminders and always
giving thanks, too.
Gave her strength and reminded her of what to do.
She loved her family deeply from the heart
Children, sister, and cousins occupied a special part.
An intimate relationship with her mom she had,
Always sought her advice even when she was mad.
When she dealt with difficulties of one kind or another,
She always said "I'm calling my mother."
Her joys and pains she openly shared,
Expressed to others how much she cared.
Though no one ever wants to experience loss and grief,
The hope of looking again into my daughter's eyes
Is a comforting relief.

Parent's Reflection

Joyous relief when the baby is born;
Feelings of pride when graduation caps are worn;
Worrisome thoughts when they move out on their own;
Hoping they will be careful and always answer their phone.
Though all grown up, always want to be there;
Reminiscing viewing photos of every moment, every year.
Suddenly all that is left is the memory.
Life not the same with part of the heart empty.

The Wound That Will Not Heal – A Mother's True Story

I read some time, ago, the loss of a child is the most difficult to bear,
I never thought the words "your daughter died" I would hear.
Receiving the first call she was in ICU and not well,
Then I heard her voice, she was afraid, I could tell.
I spoke with her calmly and told her to relax and breath slow,
You see, her respiration was high and oxygen very low.

Her sister and I visited every day,
It was uncertain at first but then she was doing okay.
Though feeling better and looking good
Her lungs were still recovering, we understood.

On a Monday afternoon when I visited
She said they lowered her oxygen and she was excited.
The next morning she and I communicated by text,
I told her I would not be there that day but the next.
She said no problem, mummy I love you
I sent her the same with an emoji too.

Later that day a nurse called about her breathing,
She was having difficulty with heavy wheezing.
I spoke with her and told her to keep on the mask,
Her lungs needed oxygen to complete its' task.
A lot calmer, she said okay and good night,
but a few hours later, I received a call - she was not alright.
I drove to the hospital at 2:30 while still dark out,
fearful of what this was really about.
In a small room, what I was told was confusing and not so detailed,

I could not speak but felt someone or something failed.
When I walked in her room, I did not receive the
usual cheerful "hi!"
And when I called her name there was no reply.
Always I seek help and support through prayer,
Though there alone, I was confident he was there.

Seeing a ventilator tube replace her bright smile,
Feeling physically weak, a friend's number I began to dial.
Sitting with phone to ear and friend on the other end,
A nurse rushed in and chose this time to deeply offend.
She walked in with a bag, started to remove her belongings
and pack,
Struggling to hold back tears, I asked her to put everything
back.

Though my daughter experienced respiratory distress,
And unfortunately this led to cardiac arrest.
Though the nurse treated her as non-existent,
I knew my daughter was feisty and persistent.

Fast forwarding through two weeks, visiting every day,
My younger daughter and I interacted with her in every way.
We played music, spoke to her and gave her a regular
massage,
Hopeful her eyes would open, we posted a family picture
collage.

The medical team said she was alive with brain activity,
But her future would be as a young woman with some form
of disability
They still suggested to discontinue the vent and would not

give up,
Until I firmly stated her supported breathing, I would not interrupt.

This is how and when the wound first occurred,
From the entry to ICU until an acute hospital she was transferred.
Initially, this felt like a sudden and sharp jab,
as though someone reached in and gave my heart a stab.
To further deepen the pain, she was sent two hours away,
I questioned perhaps not enough did I pray?
I did not know for critical cases the hospital was renowned,
My confidence was strengthened in how this place was found.

The hospital was for those in need of acute care,
To what extent she would be helped, I was not aware.
Until one day I walked in and she was awake!
Gradually transitioned off the vent and removal of the trachea.
During one visit, the therapist asked, "Who is this you see?"
My daughter looked at me and said, "It's mummy!"

Her recovery was amazing, almost unreal,
Now my wound had started to heal,
I set up my laptop in her room,
So she could see and talk to the family on Zoom.

She wanted to leave and devised an escape plan,
She said, "Mummy, just take me out for a ride in your van."
With the speech therapist she started eating ice then applesauce.
While PT and OT helped with weakness and muscle loss.

It became time for her to move on to a rehabilitation center,
It was not easy to find as many said she was too young to enter.
The case Manager gave me a list and she worked on one too,
Though a bit frustrating, one finally came through.
I read the website and scheduled a tour,
It seemed okay, but how could one be absolutely sure.
I was told either a facility farther away or there she had to go,
Other places willing to accept her had waitlists that moved slow.

The experience in the rehabilitation and healthcare center is too much to tell,
Within four months she was twice sent to the hospital, one time because she fell.
The other visit to the hospital, she was transferred to ICU,
I felt we were repeating what we had already been through.
My healing wound re-opened and became inflamed,
The center did not hold to the quality of care they proclaimed.

I pleaded for her not to return to the same place,
However, there was no facility that had bed space.
My daughter returned to the facility, despite how hard I tried,
And six weeks later in their facility she died.

My wound was now severely infected
whole body ached, even with cortisone injected.
Daily I functioned routinely in a thick fog
Traumatized with memories I could not unclog.

What I will say next is not a cliche but true,
It's only because of God I am making it through.
On my own, every day I would desperately dread,
But he gave me strength, friends, and things to do instead.
The loss of and the way I lost my daughter was a harrowing ordeal,
I labeled it, the wound that will not heal.

I could have a wonderful week through Saturday night,
Then wake up Sunday mornings not feeling right.
Around 7:30, the wound aches reminding me it's still there,
It was the day and time I received the words no parent wants to hear.
It is absolutely astonishing how we were created,
Physically, emotionally, psychologically all interrelated.

I can hide my wound, with my emotions concealed,
Without anyone knowing it has not yet healed.
While a physical wound should be properly bandaged,
This wound, to keep covered, would cause more damage.

There are times I want to repeatedly reveal the wound to friends and family,
But I don't want to burden anyone and they feel I need attention frequently.
Do I really think they would feel that way?
Perhaps it's my overthinking that sometimes goes astray.
But one thing of which I am sure,
I have a family of friends with whom I feel secure.
And poetry has allowed me to descriptively reveal,
the true story behind the wound that will not heal....
Yet.

Under My Favorite Tree

Sitting on a bed of grass under my favorite tree,
Enjoying life unafraid as I sip on my ice tea.

On the park bench, sat a handsome man with beautiful eyes,
I couldn't focus on my writing as his familiar face I analyzed.
I couldn't help but ask, excuse me sir, what is your name?
He said some call me Jimmy but to most I am James.
I jumped quickly to my feet and my heart beat sped up too,
This was really daddy alive and body brand new.

Overcome with emotion my legs became like tires without air,
Just as when I was a little girl, he said it's okay, I'm here.
My daddy then held me in his warm strong embrace,
Under my favorite tree, the perfect place.

We talked while sharing a late afternoon lunch,
Like a little girl I told him I missed him a whole bunch.
Then my father said, Angie, take a look behind the tree,
There were my brothers, alive, all three!
They just kept coming, one after another, nephews, nieces, aunts, grandfathers and grandmothers!

We hugged, cried, and sat under the tree for a while,
The overwhelming finale was the arrival of my mother and oldest child.
All of this took place around and under my favorite tree,
Sitting alone writing then reunited with all of my family.

FROM WITHIN

One Day I'll Dance Again

When I was young I loved to dance,
Shy and much too young for romance.
No anxious heart or troubled mind,
No pressures or tension of any kind.
I closed my eyes as the music filled my head
House full of people but heard no words said.
Lost in a tranquil world of my own,
No shame or fear dancing alone.
Though I and life have changed since then,
I know, like before, one day I'll dance again.

The Five Day Ramble

Day 1
The expiration date on the smoked turkey was January 21,
The same month and day when my daughters' life had begun.

Day 2
Searching for my name and a place,
A seat I can claim and embrace.

Day 3
Some memories floating through my mind,
Summaries of people I can no longer find.

Day 4
Feeling the cold through my seams,
While on the road to get ice cream.

Day 5
Why did I allow myself to get into this mess,
A Thoughtless invitation to unnecessary distress.

Ice Cream and my Locked Door

The ice cream and my locked door,
The connection, by the end you'll know for sure;
Single life now, feels so different
Staying busy and learning to be content,
Children grown up, all on their own.
Adjusting to the new, living alone.
It is night but I will be alright,
bought ice cream for only one at the store,
enjoyed it at home, safe behind my locked door.

The Change

What's happening to me
I am no longer the same
Where is the person I used to be
there's no change in my name.
My body moves differently
Is illness, stress, or age to blame?
I do not walk as confident and freely,
At times assisted by my friend cane.
Many nights I lie in bed sleeplessly,
Before, I fell asleep until morning came.
Many mornings my body feels achy,
As the mind plays what day is it game.
I don't like what's happening to me
Nor this changed body I now claim.
But this is my present reality
To embrace with grace, not shame.

Transforming Me

Time to re-do me,
It's not so easy.
Daily I try hard
Bad habits to discard.
Still making mistakes
does life have retakes?
I'm transforming me.

The inside conflict,
I'm my own convict.
With each step I go,
Weakness follows.
Fear of changing,
Life rearranging.
I'm transforming me.

A hand extended,
Help recommended.
Accepted it all,
to prevent a fall.
A brand-new feeling,
Each day revealing.
I'm transforming me.

My Tsunami

Emotions held deep
into my heart.
As I swallow,
my tongue is like a dry seabed.
The moisture rose
in slow motion,
behind unblinking eyes,
held steady
with a wide stare.
.
My mind and my heart
Was confused.
What the mind tried to stop
The heart wanted to do.
I felt the sensation of an eruption
The feeling climbed up slowly,
Taking hostage of my heart.
My throat stung
I started to gasp for breath.
My body trembled and
I was overcome with weakness.

There was no escape.
waves of forced water
poured from my face.
My lips parted
and produced an explosive roar.
This is my cry, my tsunami.

My Parents

Daddy's love for his family was incredibly strong;
He taught us well, the sense of right and wrong.

When we think of mommy, how truly blessed we were;
She was a loving and self-sacrificing mother all of us concur.
While Daddy worked hard, she was our at home mom;
Seeing us off to school, always busy, but calm.

Every morning, daddy walked to take the train on a dark quiet street;
to his full-time job, making sure we always had plenty to eat.
He took very good care of his children and wife;
He worked hard to provide us the best life.

Mommy made us well during our colds, pains, and fevers;
When we tried to fake illness, we could not deceive her.
Excellent cook and baker, for her there was no match;
Every meal and dessert was made only from scratch.

Structured and consistent was the schedule during the week day;
But the weekend was for family togetherness, fun, and play.
A schedule of recreation was a life enriching touch;
Bowling, skating, movies, amusement parks – but never too much.

I remember on Saturday evenings of food, dancing, and singing in harmony;
Daddy was a music man and he was expert in finding the right key.

Our parents loved to dance, especially the dance of swing;
We were their awestruck audience, clapping and cheering.
It was not until after their death we learned something we did not know;
Daddy was a ballroom dancer and his lead mommy elegantly followed.

Daddy was a good husband and father, mommy a beautiful wife and mother;
If we could rewind and start life again, I would want the same parents, no other.

Mama Angela

By two beautiful girls I was given this name,
certainly not because of regality or fame.
But these girls are loving, respectful, and kind.
Though not related, they're like granddaughters of mine.
They will never walk by without a hug and sweet hello,
Not only me but to everyone they know.
Spending time with the girls is always a pleasure,
And my relationship with them, I'll aways treasure.

Family

Many songs exist today,
Describing family this or that way.
But the real meaning lies individually inside,
If within the heart love does genuinely reside.
It is revealed in what we say and do,
Demonstrating clearly the words I love you.
Sometimes words exchanged may not feel nice
Resentment not permitted, a simple apology would suffice.
When communication is not always about us;
But about the other person and many positive things we
could discuss.
Doing our part to maintain peace and not divide;
Being a true friend to each other we can trust and confide
Through all the sad, the bad and the good,
Thinking about family members first as we should.
Now let's personalize, and examine how it applies.
Do we have a parent though older still alive?
Are we doing our best to help them peacefully survive?
Do we provide for their needs, regularly visit and call?
Or do we spare little time, because our lives are so busy, after
all.
How would we feel if they should no longer exist?
This wonderful opportunity now we would have missed.
That would be such a shame,
Left with tears and only ourselves to blame.

My Gold Standard Onion

Green, red, or yellow, the gold standard onion is the best,
Like you, my kind of fellow, a step above the rest.
Unlike your skin, I was like winter squash not easy to peel,
I was captured by your looks but more needed to be revealed.
I used to fear the onion because of the burning and tearing of my eyes,
I learned techniques to prevent the effect, with you the same would apply.
Sometimes a person can cry from the gold onion's high sulfur content,
From what I learned about you there is nothing harmful to that extent.
As cool water running over the onion, I presented myself that way to you,
Not moving too fast, using wisdom as a sharp knife to discerningly cut through.
Like the onion cut up and all exposed, so much about you was disclosed.
Satisfied with my observation one hundred percent
like the onion in the pan, the final test you underwent.
As the onion becomes sweet and mild when it is sauteed,
A positive attitude and good qualities you displayed.
My gold standard onion, to me you are the best,
though there are many varieties available, I choose you over the rest.

An Ancient King

What would it have been like to be there with a particular ancient king?
a solo audience, in suspense, a witness to everything.

Hidden in a front row section of bushes during the battles they won,
or observing from an aerial view when he and his men were on the run.

Would I have been one of the many women in complete awe,
of his strength, beauty, skills, and loyalty to Supreme law?

Or would I have found it difficult to remain respectful and loyal to a king,
who secretly desired a woman who wore another man's ring?

Though an appointed ruler he was human and made mistakes,
He composed songs that revealed his regrets and heartaches.

What would it have been like to be there with this particular ancient king?
To observe and learn from his example would have been an amazing thing.

My Strength

I seek and thirst for you.
In my life you are first - or who?
Else has the power when I'm weak to infuse,
Absolutely no one could fill your shoes.
Like a speedy ambulance, my helper you are,
when I feel afraid I remember you're never too far.
I'm in absolute awe with your strength and beauty,
To live with full devotion, I can never be off duty.
As your right hand holds me steady, to you tightly I cling,
even during hard times, I'm confident of what the future
will bring.

Retirement

Contemplating retirement can induce depression and fear,
Wondering what to do with so much time to spare,
Reflecting on a life, empty and full of despair.
Focus on what you should do and not what will be
hard to bear,
Such as your mental and physical health, be sure to
take good care.
Do not spend too much time sitting in a comfortable chair,
But go for daily walks out in the open air.
It's okay to grieve the loss and even shed a tear,
But be sure to create a new schedule daily to adhere,
Stay busy, active, associate, and volunteer,
Help others and your experience freely share.

Music

Magnetic, **u**niversal, **s**timulating,
influential, **c**aptivating.
Host of emotions can start stirring.
happiness, sadness, right and wrong desire,
Beats and repetition excite and inspire.
But be careful of its' artful power,
encouraging good but the good it can devour.
It is wise to be cautious and selective,
If needed, take action that is corrective.
Music is a unique and beautiful gift to appreciate,
listen to, dance to, and with vocals or instruments create.

The Past

I am all of what you used to be,
I am the best and worst in your memory.
Our start was when you were born
that morning, afternoon, or night,
When you were delivered then examined
to make sure you were alright.
Day care to high school, graduations too,
I was there recording it all for you.
I can be your good friend or foe,
As everything about you I know.
Fun and exciting things about me you love to tell,
Then there are parts of me you wish you could expel.
There may be things about me that cause you to feel shame,
But those feelings also contribute to the individual you
became.
Unfortunately, there's no part of me you can permanently
delete,
Then too, anything we did together, you never have to repeat.
And beware of dwelling on our good days for too long,
Discontentment with present living can grow strong.
I am as powerful as you allow me to be,
You, not I, have control over me.
At any time you can leave me with no need to return,
Cherish the good, dismiss the bad, value the lessons learned.
Remember, who you are at present, I will shortly be,
What you do now, I will become a pleasant or regrettable
memory.

Just Feeling Neutral

Ever wake up not feeling happy, not feeling sad,
Not excited about the day, but not mad,
No particular thought bad or good,
Not sure if you feel appreciated or misunderstood.
Need to get out of the bed
Prefer to stay under the covers instead.
Don't worry, the feeling might not be crucial,
But one of those days you're just feeling neutral.

My Favorite Song

Of my many favorite songs, it's hard just one to choose,
In two different languages, I fell in love with the wording
used.

In my mother tongue, it is full of meaning,
But, toward the foreign language my heart was leaning.

You see, the two versions of the song are exactly the same
rhythmically,
But the other language is more descriptive touching my heart
specifically.

A Lightning Lesson

The sudden arrival of an incredible thought,
is like lightning striking when air is momentarily searing hot.
Like being stunned by lightening, eyes wide and gazing,
is the excitement of words, ideas, images, sparking and blazing.
Then there are thoughts that become lightning and have a tazing effect,
But like a remote control, a change of thought the mind can select.
The lightning's charge can damage trees, buildings, even people,
I ask myself, at times, are my words to others electrically charged and lethal?
And did you know, lightning produces thunder?
The booming sound that startles, and living things look for cover to hide under.
When conversing with others, am I the loudest sound in nature, I wonder.
But there is a lot of good in lightning often unseen,
such as working to make our environment green.
It contributes to the feel of fresh air while reducing odor,
This reminds me to do my part as a peace promoter.

I Listened to a Song

I listened to a song with no words but much to say.
A melody of voices that struck me in a particular way.
Like the sudden and gradual darkness of a coming storm
Deeply painful thoughts without warning began to form.
I was unsure of how the end would be,
questioning if the song would overtake me.
Yes, I listened to a song today,
Had no words but much to convey.
The plaintive blend of vocal sound reached a crescendo,
Like the deep ache in my heart seeking an emotional plateau.
The depth of my emotions it precisely described.
Finally a comprehension of my sadness had arrived.
With my face wet with tears I listened to the song again and again,
experiencing the freedom of not needing to pretend.

The Truth vs. The Lie

Stable, faithful, based on facts
Traceable, graceful, stays on track
Firm, unites, non-competitive
affirms, invites, transformative

Fable, swayful, consistency lacks,
Inflatable, painful, preys and attacks
Squirms, ignites, always divisive
disaffirms, slights, and resistive.

In sync no not ever
But bring the two together
the truth helps you clearly see,
the lie you can detect easily.

My Fork in the Road

Lights, camera, action! Wait, pause and rewind!
This is really about the time I almost lost my mind.
It started with the school of cosmetology,
An alternative to support my volunteer service strategy
Employed at the same job for a few years,
An unexpected meeting, resulted in suddenly shifting gears.
Yes, laid off due to a budget cut,
Prayerfully changed professions to prevent a financial rut.

The school environment was unanticipated,
What the ears perceived all day, the brain struggled to eliminate it.
Worked hard, asked questions as I usually do,
Instructors thought lots in store for me to pursue.
Before graduation there was a fashion show.
Presented my skills on the models' head to toe.
Finished with school, with certificate and license at last!
Surprised at the conclusion with awards I amassed.

One day while reading a fashion magazine's latest edition,
I learned of a big event, an international competition.
Yes, I entered and it consumed a lot of my time,
I loved the world of beauty, hair, make-up, and fashion design!
Photographs taken of the models before and after,
Intense at times also with lots of laughter.
I was disappointed I did not win,
Though I promised I was done, I did it again!
My time, thinking, and skills swallowed up whole,

My dear sister coworker told me I was out of control.
No, this is what I enjoy, just having fun,
But my so called perfect schedule was completely undone.
This was not just about traveling to London, performing, and winning.
This was a weakness that had my entire life spinning.
When you're caught into this whirlwind, you cannot always see,
The drifting that happens and to what degree.
This world of beauty within me produced a natural high,
Was it worth saying to all and everything important to me good-bye?
This was my fork in the road, I hope others benefit from the story I told.

I Wish I Said

Residual thoughts in my head
of some things I wish I said.
I wish I said no instead of yes,
not settled for so much less.
I wish I said yes and not no,
missed opportunities and places to go.
I wish I said I don't know when I was not sure,
some decisions and choices made were poor
I wish I said why rather than let things be,
remaining silent though I did not agree.
Residual thoughts in my head
of some things I wish I said.

Uninvited

There was this exciting event,
I was invited, but never went.
By telephone, I was asked to attend,
The invitation perhaps they forgot to send.

I should just go, I rationalized,
After all, I have associational ties.
What if on the guest list my name they cannot find,
That would surely be most embarrassing and unkind.

My pride still intact, I chose not to go,
I did have a chance to see pictures though.
Beautiful bright smiles, always delightful to see,
Clothing and hairstyles, all sharp I had to agree.

Though this event happened long ago
It was an opportunity for me to grow:
Whether it is a verbal or written notice to all invited,
There will be someone who is or feels slighted.
I've discovered, when it's time for the final guest count,
Usually, it becomes necessary to decrease the amount.

So, whether I am a guest, the uninvited or the host,
I keep in mind it's love that matters most.

The Best GPS

Everywhere, every place I follow my GPS,
Guides my vehicle through the traveling process.
Without it, put simply I would be in a mess,
following my own directions as a solo adventuress.
this way often leads to frustration and distress.
But I found a GPS that is the absolute best,
one that always leads me to success,
A reliable and important compass,
available in many languages with ease of access.
Regular users agree it is the best GPS.

Hi, How Are You?

After a "Hi" or a "Hello"
How are you? immediately follows.
Am I really interested in a reply,
Or is it an extension of my greeting as I pass by?
I need to be sure if it's genuine
Whether to someone I just met or a friend.
It has become a habit and not a good one at all
Whether in person or during a phone call.
The next time I speak with a Hi! or Hello!
Concern for others I will strive to show,
After my greeting, I'll pause then ask how are you?
Since I sincerely want to know, I will listen too.

I Did Not Hug You Today

I was in a hurry and said a quick hello,
Running late or had somewhere to go.
At a short distance I formed a quick smile,
I was not aware of your most recent trial.
So many people to speak to and things to do,
I did not realize I often walk silently by you.
One day, in my usual rush, I noticed you standing alone,
It occurred to me I did not attempt to reach you by phone,
Then my heart nudged me, reminding of the most loving
way,
Arms open wide, I approached you and said, "I did not hug
you today."

The White Shorts

Chubby, fatso, even butterball,
back in the day some of us were called it all.
But it really didn't bother me too much,
who I was on the inside no one could touch.

The biggest problem was finding clothes to fit,
Especially pants as they could easily split.
Like most my age I liked to dress nice,
But, slightly larger clothing was at a higher price,
There was a boutique in town that had a "chubby" section,
Trendy and in style clothing they had a good selection.

As for money, well, my parents had to pay a lot more,
But the clothing quality was the best in this store.
One day there were these white shorts on the rack,
One look at the price and I put them right back.
As usual I would try on clothes in the dressing room
Might be my size, but one can never assume.

When I thought I was finished my mother would bring more,
Handing items I might like over the dressing room door.
I appreciated my mother's patience, style and good taste,
Never once did she feel the time spent was a waste.
Suddenly she handed me the white shorts without a word,
My brain in wild surprise could not believe what just
occurred.
I put one leg in and then the other, If they'll fit, I would
soon discover.
Please make it beyond the hips without being too tight,
Now button, then zip, not too short, they fit just right!

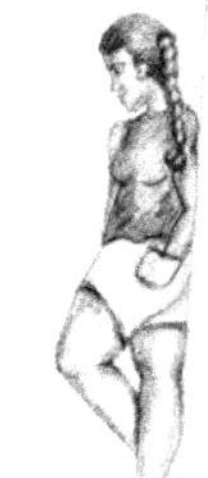

Though my beautiful white shorts are long gone,
I'll never forget that special moment when I tried them on.

My Minaudiere

Like my pocketbook, where I go you're always there,
close to me whether I'm feeling good or in despair.
More important than a cosmetic case or purse,
by my side all the roads you traversed,
Like my wallet, losing you, would stir intense fear.
So much more valuable, you are my minaudiere,
Some sparkle with gold or are embellished with stones,
But like platinum, you stand alone.
My reason for holding on to you is defensible,
Because you are without a doubt indispensable.
My expressions about you are all sincere.
You are my one and only minaudiere.

Shades On!

There were two lovely ladies named Laynah and Shay,
A wide gap in age but they accessorized the same way.
So very particularly about how they dressed,
Before going out always wanted to look their best.
Colorful, coordinated, or matched to perfection,
Then a look in the mirror for the final inspection.
One wore chap stick the other light gloss on the lips,
Hair styled just so, at times with hair barretts or clips.
And never did they leave without a pocketbook,
This complemented but not yet completed the look.
Ears, neck, and hands with jewelry artistically displayed on,
The final touch was when they put their Shades On!

Curtains

A piece of material that can decorate or divide,
It also has the ability to darken or hide.
And by the way, did you know,
An ancient book described their use long ago?
Today some curtains are made of fine linen or lace,
In beautiful colors to dress up any window, shower,
or closet space.
From semi-sheer, pleated, priscilla, and brocade,
to toppers, valances, swags, and balloon shades.
I've noticed many opt for a bare window,
I guess they don't mind everything inside all will know.
Some prefer decorating windows with blinds,
Horizontal, vertical, there are many kinds.
I grew up with every window fashioned with a shade and
curtain,
though I now prefer blinds, material frames my window for
certain!

The Idiosyncratic Instrument

The piano, violin, brass which instrument?
Well let's talk about one a bit different.
There are no keys, strings, sticks, or hinges
Look down on your face about four to six inches.
Yes, this is called vocal percussion,
Making music with your mouth is the topic of discussion.
The art of creating sound or imitating an instrument,
Not a new concept but naturally brilliant.
Producing the realistic beat of a drum,
Or a soothing sound, and this is profound, with a closed mouth hum?
Remember in the 1980s the infectious beat boxing,
vocal percussion and spoken word cleverly interlocking.
And what about doodle-lee-dee-be-dah, shoo-bee-doo,
The introduction of scat by the great jazz, and blues singers too.
Yes, our idiosyncratic musical instrument,
Learned and played for years without a penny spent.

THE CHILD IN ME

I Saw Turkeys Fly in the Tree

It was a cloudy and rainy day.
Mom said I could not go out and play.
I asked mom, "Will the rain stop soon?"
Mom said, "I don't know, maybe by noon.

Then I thought, I know what to do,
I will wait by the window until the
Sky turns blue.
I sat and sat but still no sun.
Inside all day is just no fun.

But wait, what is that I see?
Not one turkey, not two, but there are three.
"Mom, mom, come quickly!"
There are three big turkeys flying in
the tree!"

Mom looked and said, "oh my, I did not know turkeys
could fly!"
I said, "Wow, look mom there is one more!"
There were three turkeys now there are four!"

At first, I was sad I could not go outside to play,
But I saw turkeys fly in the tree and I had a
good day.

My Granddaughter's Dream

She arrived in the middle of nowhere,
a darkened room with bright lights everywhere.

There was a staircase glistening like an ice-skating rink,
A brilliant metallic hue with specks of bright pink.
At each corner, guards stood with gloved hands,
As music played by four different bands.

As she fought to open her eyes to force herself awake,
the entertaining scene became a lovely wedding cake.

Will I Be Okay

Will I be okay so you ask me
I'll be okay in just a while,
Is it the environment,
Maybe my temperament
Or emotional imprisonment.
Please no judgment.
Will I be okay so you ask me
I'll be okay in just a while.

Let's Work It Out

Married life can be incredibly difficult
but with love and effort come good results.

So let's just work it out
What's it really all about
No need to argue or shout.
We can't leave respect out.

Hurt feelings can get in the way
Of what we really want to say
Instead of stubborn pride
Let's talk and apologize.

A happy life can include tears
but still enjoy life together for years

So, let's work it out
What's it really all about
No need to argue or shout
We can't leave respect out.

Anxious About

Anxious about yesterday,
today, and tomorrow
Anxious about you, me
And what follows.
Can't help being anxious about.

Alone in My Room

Sitting on my comfortable bed,
staring at the ivory wall;
not feeling any dread,
no texting no phone call.

Staring at the ivory wall,
thinking about the long day;
no texting no phone call,
my favorite song starts to play.

Thinking about the long day,
outside is the dark night;
my favorite song starts to play
the light inside is bright.

Outside is the dark night,
not feeling any dread;
the light inside is bright,
sitting on my comfortable bed.

I Read It

I read it
Couldn't stop myself
Now I regret it
Words now in my mind lingering
Without notice has me staggering.
I read it
I said I would not
Now I can't forget it.
I knew but didn't want to know,
Now it's inside with nowhere to go
I read it
Couldn't stop myself
Now I regret it.
I could delete or shred it,
Still in my mind it is embedded.
Maybe one day I will forget it.
But I read it.
Couldn't stop myself
Now I regret it.
Because I read it.

I Remember

The sun played happily in the sky,
until the moon kissed everyone goodbye.
the sweet sound of the words, "I do"
the dance with the soft whisper, "I love you."
Then the sun seemed to slowly disappear,
and the moon, shed its' very first tear.
Remember the initial sun and moon?
In love and dancing to a favorite tune.
I Remember.

A POETIC SHORT STORY

Atawa's Cry

She had become so tired of her own facade,
Always hiding the truth that life for her was hard.
It began when she was a child,
always presented as quiet and mild.

An honor roll student, classmates called her an overachiever,
She was proud of her grades though they laughed and teased her.
This did not bother her much, so she thought,
until their friendship she wanted and sought.
Often she was given the cold shoulder,
You're the teacher's pet they always told her.
This was life in school through junior high,
Until she finished 8th grade and said good-bye.

The high-school years were busy and sped by fast,
But that's when Atawa discovered the use of a mask.
In the 12th grade, she lost her grandmother and dad,
Though close with her mom, she felt she lost all she had.
Her friends in school did not attend the funeral,
But Atawa made excuses for them, as usual.
No comforting words, not even a hug,
on Atawa's heart this was a painful tug.
Atawa swallowed her feelings, dismissed it, and wore a smile,
Kept up with school work and friendship pretenses for a while.

At last, graduation day finally came,
Though with honors, there was no fame.

The speakers explained, there was so much you could achieve,
With dedication, hard work, and in yourself you believe.
Atawa thought, isn't this what I've been doing?
As the past 12 years her mind was reviewing.
With a diploma, an award, and scholarship she went home,
Couldn't wait to change clothes and be in her room alone.

Atawa worked hard toward achieving her Bachelor's degree,
However, the unexpected happened at the end of year three.
At the end of each semester, she made the dean's list,
Alert and focused, not a class or assignment missed.
Atawa was confident and excited about her last year,
Until one night her elation suddenly transformed into fear.
What was happening to her, she did know,
Her body running to an escape with no where to go.
Her entire being was in an extreme state of alarm,
As if someone or something was attempting to cause her harm.
Body trembling from the inside out, she was in distress, there was no doubt.
Heart beating fast and strong, eyes stretched wide,
Atawa wondered if and when this episode would subside.

Atawa called her mother who told her to breath in a brown paper bag, the small size,
This seemed to help a lot to control the breathing, to Atawa's surprise.
The calmness of her mother's voice helped slow down her heart rate,
Though relieved, Atawa felt badly about an urgent call so late.
Atawa finally fell asleep in the morning's dark night,

She felt safe surrounded by the glow of her bedroom light.

Atawa's doctor told her she had an anxiety or panic attack,
It would be helpful to slow down and take time to relax.
The next year was not so easy, Atawa felt the struggle,
The demands of work, school, and bills she had to juggle.
The attacks continued, always leaving her feeling alone and afraid, but on the outside and to the public she never displayed.

Finally, Atawa obtained her degree, and was given a promotion,
Her boss said she was an asset to the team and he appreciated her devotion.
During lunch break, smiling on the inside and taking it all in, she was startled by a voice that said, "Hey beautiful, where have you been?"
Atawa quickly looked up at this handsome man with an appealing smile,
She couldn't resist saying, "I have not heard such a corny line like that in a while."
The two laughed together and dating soon began,
Atawa felt attracted to the caliber of this man.
About a year later they had an intimate wedding,
With family and friends in a simple elegant setting.

It was not easy adjusting to marital life,
But Atawa really wanted to be a good wife.
She was so thankful she learned to cook from her mother and grandmom,
Because after work her husband appreciated a home-cooked meal ready and warm.

One evening though, when he was unusually late,
this sent Atawa into an uncontrollable anxious state.
When he walked in and saw Atawa's panic stricken face
He yelled out what happened as he held her in a tight warm embrace.
He asked if he should call an ambulance, but Atawa said, "No!"
"This has happened before the symptoms will soon go.",
Atawa apologized that she did not share this before now.
he said, "I am your husband, we're in this together, remember our vow?"
To cry until the morning in his arms is all Atawa wanted to do,
Instead she looked in his sincere eyes and said, "I truly love you."
Atawa did not want to reveal that she became afraid he would not return,
As when she was a child, her father did not come home after work, but he died, she later learned.

Atawa did not sleep well thinking about the words of her husband,
she knew she had to share a lot more with the man she adored and trusted in.
She smiled thinking about their talk about having children was a future maybe,
However, little did they know that only a few months later
Atawa would be expecting a baby.

A little disappointed, somewhat confused,
Slightly sad, mostly amused.

In Atawa's mind, heart, and life she was making room,
For the first precious life growing in her womb.
The months seemed to have skipped days, as time quickly sped by,
After exhausting hours of labor, Atawa gave birth, and heard their little girl's first cry.

It was not easy working from home and taking care of a child,
But Atawa adjusted well after a short while.
They appreciated and looked forward to Fridays from five to eight,
When her mother-in-law babysat so they could enjoy a dinner date.
On Saturdays Atawa visited her mother for time to spend with her only grandchild and daughter,
She did not miss a weekend with her mother and it made her happy to observe the joy it brought her.

However, Atawa received an alarming call one Saturday,
Her mother had a heart attack, she needed to get to the hospital right away.
Her in-laws met them there and when all arrived,
Atawa was shocked to learn her mother did not survive.

Portrayal of a woman always resilient and strong.
Concealed emotions held in for too long,
As the weight of it felt staggering and too much to bear,
Atawa felt her husband's hand gently wipe away a tear.
With no room left inside to store the heaviness of this pain,
Held tightly in his arms, she cried like a storm of thunder and rain.

Back to her regular routine and after a few months had passed,
Home alone, Atawa wondered how long her grieving would last.
As a sudden downpour of rain from a darkened charcoal sky,
Throughout the day, Atawa would unexpectedly cry.
While she loved her husband and daughter, with no complaints as a mother and wife,
The troubling thought in her mind was about the brevity and purpose of life.
Filled with sadness and anxiety, sitting on her living room floor,
Atawa was startled by a sudden knock on the front door.

(To be continued)

ABOUT THE AUTHOR

Angela Ruth began writing poetry at the age of sixteen. She discovered an outlet to reveal her thoughts and emotions on paper. Angela continued writing until her early twenties, however, when she moved to a different area of the city, two notebooks full of her original poetry was mistakenly left behind. When she realized they were left behind, she returned to inquire about the notebooks, however, the new tenants said they threw them away. Angela was devastated and did not write for a few years. Later, she again began to explore the art of poetry, including creatively using the imagination, and developing her own style. She facilitated a six-week poetry group at her place of employment and the group created a non-published collection of poems.

While writing another book is not a near future plan, Angela will utilize Instagram (@angruthela to periodically feature new writings.

www.ingramcontent.com/pod-product-compliance
Lightning Source LLC
LaVergne TN
LVHW020654100826
845148LV00012B/2493

* 9 7 9 8 2 1 8 9 2 8 5 0 6 *